Rivka Galchen had never been interested in babies or motherhood. But suddenly, when her daughter was born, everything seemed directly related to them. *Little Labours* is a slanted, enchanted miscellany prompted by her newly overturned life.

She writes about babies in art and babies in literature; about the effort of taking a passport photo for a baby not yet able to hold up her head and the frightening prevalence of orange as today's chic colour for baby gifts; about Frankenstein as a sort of baby and a baby as a sort of Godzilla.

In this memoir quite unlike any other, Galchen opens up an odd and tender world.

Little Labours

Rivka Galchen

Little Labours

4th ESTATE • *London*

4th Estate
An imprint of HarperCollins*Publishers*
1 London Bridge Street
London SE1 9GF
www.4thEstate.co.uk

First published in Great Britain in 2017 by 4th Estate
First published in the United States by New Directions in 2016

1

"Notes on Some Twentieth-Century Writers" originally
appeared in *Harper's Magazine*.

A catalogue record for this book is
available from the British Library.

ISBN 978-0-00-822518-6

Design by Erik Rieselbach

Printed and bound in Great Britain by
Clays Ltd, St Ives plc

MIX
Paper from
responsible sources
FSC® C007454

Little Labours

Children's books

Books for young children rarely feature children. They feature animals, or monsters, or, occasionally, children behaving like animals or monsters. Books for adults almost invariably feature adults.

The crystal child

My mother tells me that people tell her, when she is out with the baby, that the baby is a crystal child. Some people ask for permission to touch the baby, because contact with crystal children is healing. "You should research what it is, crystal children," my mother, who has a master's degree in computer science and an undergraduate degree in mathematics, says more than once. From the moment my mother first met the baby, she found her to be an exceptional and superior creature; her ascribing of crystal child qualities to the baby is part of this ongoing story.

I finally go ahead and research crystal children. On the Web. I learn that, unlike rainbow children, crystal children have a difficult time because they believe they can change the way people think in order to heal the world; rainbow children by contrast understand that people cannot be changed, they can only be loved as they are; rainbow children are therefore less frustrated than crystal children. Crystal children were born, one site explains, mostly in the nineties, whereas rainbow children arrived, by and large, in the new millennium—prior to the generation of crystal children there was a generation of indigo children—and so maybe the puma is in fact a rainbow child, rather than a crystal child, or maybe she is part of an even newer generation, as yet uneponymized.

Maybe in the same way that children in the Middle Ages who were born with congenital hypothyroidism (as was common before salt was iodized because iodine is essential to thyroid development) had a certain look, and were mentally different from the mainstream, and were referred to as *chrétiens*—a term which unfortunately over time became *cretins* though all it meant at the time was Christians—crystal and rainbow and indigo children are terms used mostly if not prescriptively to refer to children who are unusual in ways most commonly associated with autism or Down's syndrome.

Somehow I begin to believe in crystal children, and in the idea that my child has the special healing powers ascribed to crystal children. I start to believe this even though, unlike my mother, I don't have a master's degree in computer science, or an undergraduate degree in math. When I read one day that Isidor of Seville, back in the seventh century, was already saying that the world was round, he somehow knew so intuitively, I decide this is relevant.

But I still don't understand why no one has ever stopped *me* on the street to talk about crystal children, why they have only stopped my mother. And I don't understand why my mother, usually so suspicious of any comments made by "others," is so open to *these* comments. Someone important to me says, "It sounds like a way to love and value children who are difficult." Sure, I say, that sounds true. "Maybe your mother is telling you that she is a crystal child. Or that you are."

A long, long time ago, in late August

In late August a baby was born, or, as it seemed to me, a puma moved into my apartment, a near-mute force, and then I noticed it was December, and a movie was coming out on what is sometimes called the day of the birth of our savior. If one was to accord respect to the tetraptych poster campaign, *Forty-Seven Ronin* featured one Keanu Reeves, one robot, one monster, and one young woman dressed in green and, for unclear reasons, upside-down. The poster I kept seeing was at the end of my block, below a dance studio, around the corner from a deli next door to a Japanese clothing shop that specializes in looks inspired by American streetwear, and across the street from a dollar-a-slice pizza place perennially playing Mexican pop music. I had melatonic madness at the time. Maybe for that reason the poster, as I passed it four or five times a day, always with the puma, began to seem to really mean something, something more than what was manifest. I felt this even though I knew the poster would soon enough be replaced by one for *Vampire Academy* or the newest remake of *Robocop*, and in fact it felt almost as if that randomness-revealing replacement had already happened, as if that was part of the poster's message, that the accumulation of tomorrows was not—however lost to time I might be—going to cease producing its predictable melancholy. (However I, and I registered this as rare, I was myself at the time *not* melancholic. Not at all.) But the paradox was that as my life had become a day of unprecedented length, a day that I was calculating to now be almost three thousand hours long (in doing the math I realized that since the puma's arrival I had not slept more than 2½ hours in a row) my thoughts had become unprecedentedly interrupted, as if every three minutes I had fallen asleep, curtailing any thought, morphing it into dream, which, when I woke, was lost altogether. What I mean to say is that I wasn't working. This even though my plan had been to work. And to think. Even after the baby was born. I had imagined that I was going to meet, at birth, a very sophisticated form of plant life, a form that I would daily deliver to an offsite greenhouse; I would look forward to getting to know the life-form properly later, when she had moved into a sentient kingdom, maybe around age three. But instead, within hours of being born, the being—perhaps through chemicals the emotional-vision equivalent of smoke machines—appeared to me not like a plant at all, but instead like something much more powerfully moving than just another human being, she had appeared as an animal, a previously undiscovered old-world monkey, but one with whom I could communicate deeply: it was an unsettling, intoxicating, against-nature feeling. A feeling that felt like black magic. We were almost never apart.

I felt suddenly older, even as the puma also, in her effect on me, made me more like a very young human in one particular way, which was that all the banal (or not) objects and experiences around me were reenchanted. The world seemed ludicrously, suspiciously, adverbially sodden with meaning. Which is to say that the puma made me again more like a writer (or at least a certain kind of writer) precisely as she was making me into someone who was, enduringly, not writing.

And I really wanted to see the new forty-seven ronin movie. Even though I had no time for movies. And even though I knew there was an old version of the movie—maybe more than one old version—to which more than one person in my life had been devoted, and I always feel, and felt then, as most people do, some vague obligation to be faithful to the old, and disdainful toward the new, just as a general rule, a general rule to which I'm not deeply (or generally) opposed, even though it is stupid. But any disdain toward the new forty-seven ronin would have been superfluous anyway, since I can now tell you from this distance in time and space, that the movie that I was so ready to find meaningful was out of theaters before I ever got to see it, that it failed unambiguously in the United States and ignominiously in Japan where, despite its budget of $175 million and its popular Japanese cast and its wide release in 693 theaters—I was researching—and even its additional last-minute 3D effects and furthermore despite the fact that the base story was one which its native audience has been interested in hearing told again and again for nearly two centuries now—in Japan, the story of the forty-seven ronin is such a seminal one that there's even a special term, *chushingura*, just to describe its tellings—the movie's box office return in Japan substantially trailed that of its competitors, *Lupin the 3rd vs Detective Conan* and *The Tale of Princess Kaguya: A Princess "Crime and Punishment."*

But the poster had done its unplanned labor. A story of valiance and violence had reseeded itself into my mind and perhaps the minds of countless hungry people who had treated themselves to a slice of dollar pizza, gaze drifted to the new ronin advertised across the street.

What is a ronin? A ronin is an unemployed samurai. Or a samurai without a master. A sword for hire. The term in its time had about it something of menace or disgrace. That is no longer the case. The story of the forty-seven ronin, a few centuries old and based on a historic event and told and retold in plays and movies and honorary temple garden plaques has changed all that. The original forty-seven men (some scholars say maybe there were only forty-six) served a master who was murdered, in court, over a matter of etiquette. The murdered man's forty-seven (or forty-six) samurai were expected to avenge their master. But months passed, nothing happened. The samurai, now ronin, were said to have returned to domestic lives, or turned to drinking, or to both; it was considered shameful. But because the ronin are leading shamefully ordinary lives, the murderer of their master relaxes his guard; it appears there will be no revenge. But there will be. The ronin covertly gather, storm the compound of their master's enemy, and present his severed head to the palace. The forty-seven (or forty-six) ronin then commit self-sentenced sepukku—they are murderers now, after all—which is how their own master was coerced into ending his life as well: a symmetry. All of this is understood to be heroic (as opposed to horrifying). Honor reveals itself. In a certain way samurai resembled the wives in those cultures where the widowed are expected to throw themselves on the funeral pyre.

The story of the ronin was especially popular in the Meiji era, when Japan's isolation policy ended and power shifted from the military back to the emperor; the story was then again even more popular in the years after World War II, or so I'm told. The postwar government coerced the great filmmaker Mizoguchi, who usually made films about women in difficult circumstances, into making a movie of the forty-seven ronin, and the film's part one failed terribly, but Mizoguchi himself then wanted to make part two and did. What made the story of the forty-seven ronin so popular at those particular moments? What is the story of the forty-seven really about? A story of men who appear to be defeated and shameful, but who have elected that appearance as an essential guise for a noble plan which will become manifest? A story of violence, patience, and outsized fidelity to the master who randomly is yours?

This story is about a baby, I thought of the bloody boyish tale one afternoon, I'm not sure which afternoon, just a bright one, passing the poster with the upside-down woman as I rounded the corner past the deli. Everything was about a baby, then, but still I thought, with conviction: a baby is what the story of the forty-seven ronin is really *about*. The sleeper cell, the latent power—it's a parable about babies. They appear helpless, but they are puppetmasters. It makes so much sense. I was obviously wrong, more or less. I had been wanting, at the time of the forty-seven ronin haunting, to think on paper about, not quite coincidentally, two Japanese books: *The Pillow Book* by Sei Shonagon and *The Tale of Genji* by Murasaki Shikibu. They were two of my favorite books. It seemed mysterious to me that they both came from the same place and time, from the imperial court of early eleventh-century Japan. Both books were by women which also, I hated to admit, mattered to me. But I wasn't managing to think about either book. The puma insisted otherwise. But I didn't want to write about the puma. Mostly because I had never been interested in babies, or in mothers; in fact those subjects had seemed *perfectly* not interesting; maybe I was even repelled by mothers and babies as subjects to write about; and so, after I had the baby, I found myself in the position (now interested in babies) of those political figures who come to insights others had reached decades ago only after their personal lives intersected with an "issue," like, say, Dick Cheney, with his daughter, who married a woman. But I still didn't want to write about babies, albeit now for a different reason. I had originally wanted to write about other things because I was interested in those other things. I then specifically wanted to write about other things because that then might mean I was really, covertly, learning something about the baby, or about babies, or about being near babies, and these were subjects about which, directly, I had so little to say. In the end, without consulting me much, a cabal of neuronal circuits, ronin of their own kind, organized against me and went about coordinating their own thoughts, fueled by dollar pizza, in a minor court on 38th Street.

A *reason to apologize to friends*

All of the items pertaining to the baby are kept in a three-shelved metal cabinet in the bathroom. The cabinet is a sturdy item ordered from an industrial products catalog that also sells *Hazard* labels in bulk. On the top shelf of the cabinet, still out of the baby's reach, are diapers, crib sheets, and for no particular reason, the baby's socks. On the middle shelf of the cabinet are the baby's clothes, which are there in reasonably neatly folded piles of tops, bottoms, sweaters, and onesies. Then on the lowest shelf is whatever: hand-me-down shoes still too large, bibs never used, a swimsuit, a curling iron, too-small clothes not yet given away, and so on. But I keep the middle shelf orderly; a fair amount of effort goes into this; the orderliness of the middle shelf is a fragile, essential dam against the deluge. But the baby loves to disorder the shelves. She can't yet walk or even crawl, instead she uses her arms to heave-ho her legs forward—we call this her wounded-deer maneuver—and whenever the bathroom door is left open, she hurries (in her way) over to the cabinet and then steadily and joyfully dedicates herself to unshelving all the reachable objects, into making heaps. She is so, so happy when she does this. So happy. It is more happiness, and stuff, than one thought the cabinet could contain.

I didn't want to keep my wounded deer from her joy. But not keeping her from her joy meant that, at a later moment, usually during her rare naps, I had to go in and refold and reshelve the piles of clothes, a task that reminded me of an old Russian formalist text that baffled me when I was a college student, a text that I recall as being straightforward, and serious, and that argued for doing away with housework, since what was the point of housework, it produced nothing, it was done and then simply was started all over again, it should be abolished. Maybe that old Russian had a point. Why the shelf contained all these anxieties, I don't know, but it did. For me, it was the most important and symbolic space in the home. I was still trying to work other nonhouse-work, non-young-person-care jobs, but these attempts to work were not going well. Occasionally these things not going well combined with my general sense of being trapped inside a space that the Russian formalist of days past would have described as producing nothing and I would feel like I was turning into sand and would soon be nothing but a dispersed irritant. And so one day I decide that I will at least try to talk things over with the still-wordless wounded deer. She makes her dash toward the cabinet. I follow her. I ask her if maybe she might consider leaving the second shelf of the cabinet, the shelf with all the folded clothes on it, alone; I ask her if she would consider unshelving items only from the lowest, already disorderly, shelf. I explain to her that if she could alter her behavior in this small way, it would mean not half as much reshelving work for me, but one-tenth as much. It would be really, really nice for me, I explain. And she understands! She begins to leave the second shelf of temptingly tidily folded stacks of clothing alone. Even when unsupervised! And after that I—I tell this anecdote to friends who will listen, as if it is interesting.

What drug is a baby?

On many days I think of the baby as a drug. But what kind of a drug? One day I decide that she is an opiate: she suffuses me with a profound sense of well-being, a sense not attached to any accomplishment or attribute, and that sense of well-being is so intoxicating that I find myself willing to let my life fall apart completely in continued pursuit of this feeling. On another day, the baby calls to mind a different set and prevalence of neurotransmitters. I recall the mother of twins who said to me that, yes, she loved her girls, but one afternoon she found herself thinking with easy understanding of the woman who had drowned her five children, and she, my friend, after having that feeling decided to call for help. She called her mother. Her mother said to her, The human baby is useless, the human baby is like no other baby animal, the animals can at least walk, while the human baby is a nothing.

Dynasty

I sometimes share the elevator with a woman who is very cheerful and mean. She lives three floors above me, and so when I wait for a down elevator, I always know there is a chance she will already be on it. When we then together descend ten floors down to the lobby, she has already descended three floors—she makes one feel that. Part of what is so impressive about this neighbor of mine is that in that small box in space and time, she consistently manages to find something apt and brightly unkind to say. When I was pregnant, she said simply, "You're enormous." Another time she said, "You must be so much taller than your husband." She has a name that would have made sense for a character from *Dynasty*. She wears black almost exclusively, but a variety of blacks, blacks with such subtle variations in tactility, luminosity, and fall that one assumes they could be sold on eBay for more money than most people's rent.

When the puma arrived, Dynasty's comments shifted. "Whoa, that's a huge baby," she said, "I mean, you must be so happy." Another time, "I mean really, that's not normal, is it? Why is she so big?" This was her refrain for awhile and so I knew, more or less, what she would say before she said it, and yet still I never knew what to say back. One day I said, maybe because I was pretty sure she did not have children, and because I was not in a happy mood, "Wow, you seem to know a lot about what size babies are at what age. You know so much." It was immediately obvious that it was a defeat for me to say that, but there it was, I had already said it. Another day, I remember this was when the puma was seven months old, Dynasty said: "But she is big for her age, isn't she?" "Like me," I said. "She will be a tall person like me." Dynasty herself is not tall. Nor is she thin. I am taller and thinner than her. Yet obviously she was still winning. I had long prided myself on never being in antagonistic or competitive situations regarding size, or reproduction, or anything else really, with other women, and now here I was, I had become what I myself called the worst kind of woman, a woman who engaged with and assessed other women specifically on the level of things that had kept nearly all women down in the muck of a deforming sexual competition. Dynasty's hair has such a beautiful deep-conditioned look to it, and is very long, and though it is a mixture of gray and black, this also seems to speak only of luxury, and historic sexual power. After the tall comment, she again said of the baby's father that he was short. Another day she saw me holding a milk bottle, but without the baby, and she said, "Shouldn't they only be breastfed? Isn't that bad for them? I mean, there must be some explanation for why she's so huge. Maybe this is it." And on another day, when I had in my hand takeout from the Japanese ramen place around the corner, she said, "My god, what is that smell? Whoa, is that your food?" This was especially indicative of her sense of invincibility vis-à-vis me, as she herself is Japanese. Or maybe Chinese, or Korean; it is a private aggression on my part that I do not know, and I was devoted to continuing to not know. Not that Dynasty noticed that I didn't know.

And so it went. Each time I would go stand by the elevator, press the button, wait for the elevator's arrival, listen to the gentle ringing open of the elevator door, I would be filled with suspense. I had wasted more headspace than I could ever have imagined possible responding to an imaginary Dynasty. Yet even in the continuing expanse of time, I found I still had nothing to say. Sometimes I would imagine saying to Dynasty that it was ... interesting, what different people notice about a baby: obviously a baby is just a baby, and what people see in the baby is a reflection of themselves. Other times I would think, threateningly, My daughter is a baby now, but if you ever speak like that to my daughter when she is old enough to understand, I will destroy you. I actually think *destroy*, like in a bad movie, or middle school. Sometimes I imagine simply asking Dynasty if she has a job. She is the wife of a very wealthy man who owns and runs an advertising firm located across the street, they own the entire top floor of our building, among other things, and I feel intuitively that she could and should be ashamed of this. I know that to say any of these things would be both wrong and weak, and also that it is the weakness, rather than the wrongness, that prevents me from saying them, which only makes me more in the wrong, and more convinced that my being bothered by Dynasty at all is evidence only of my usually obscured lesser self being the real, true me.

Finally I confess to the neighbors across the hall that I have spent hours on such thoughts. Then I ask my neighbors—for some reason it matters to me—whether Dynasty has a job. They tell me that Dynasty's husband dated her for years without marrying her, that she had kept on working as a shopgirl at Commes des Garçons, that her husband still wears only Commes des Garçons, that probably she does too, that he probably refused to have kids with her, and also that they have reason to believe that the couple never has sex. I say that I understand that they are trying to turn my cartoon villain into a real person, but I tell them that I don't appreciate it, that I prefer her as a cartoon. She (not me) embodies, I decide, the evil in the world that leads to women being preoccupied by weight, fluent in cosmetics, and aspiring to be dumb muses or high-end products of choice. She is the evil beneath the cartoon Acme holes in the ground to which my daughter will be vulnerable.

But another problem with being the mother of a baby is loneliness. On many days I speak with only one adult. And for many months now, I have not seen Dynasty. Where is she? She had been so enlivening; she is so clever, and so pretty; now I am tired. I wait at the elevator, with my daughter who now walks, who pushes the button to call the elevator, who now understands the elevator, and never does the elevator door ring open to reveal our special upstairs neighbor. Each time my daughter and I are again in the hall waiting, I wait with hope. I would really like to see Dynasty again.

Cargo cult

The baby likes to stand near the toilet, tear off small pieces of paper from the toilet roll, toss them into the waters of immeasurable depth, and flush. Then repeat. A sacred ritual.

Mysteries of taste

In her ten-word *Moby-Dick* board book, she above all
loves the page that says CAPTAIN. She loves to find a
ball in a picture, especially a ball that is green or blue.
Of the six animal notecards of black and white draw-
ings, she exhibits a strong preference for Penguin. She
has not yet encountered a quantity of olives that is suf-
ficient. When she makes a scribble on paper, the result
makes her giggle. When she finds herself trapped in her
crib and wants out, she calls out to me; when I enter
the room, she says, "Eyes?" If we come upon a square or
round of metal on the sidewalk, she wants nothing more
than to stand on it, and then to go on standing there. At
other times, in the apartment, she'll set down a book,
also so as to stand on it. When she sees a bottle of milk
being poured out for her, she laughs. Little holds more
interest than a set of stairs, or a handicap-access ramp.
Always she is the first to notice the moon.

Cravings

Despite having as a child refused tomatoes, refused olives, refused mushrooms, despite having as a child been unwilling to eat anything at Chinese restaurants save the white rice, and despite having as a child made a diet nearly entirely from couscous with butter and Pepperidge Farm Chessmen cookies, and for some reason, cauliflower—an achromatic diet—despite all that, I have historically had little tolerance for finicky children. I try not to judge such children, since they are children, but in the end I find I do judge the children and I judge the parents as well, even as it was through no effort on my part that I eventually became someone who will eat most anything.

But then I became pregnant and found I was a finicky eater all over again. I was nearly unable to bear the sight or taste of much of anything save potato chips, and lemonade, and occasionally, a slice of pizza. But only low-quality pizza, the kind of pizza where the cheese seems not to have a dairy component but instead to consist exclusively of partially hydrogenated somethings. All other foods seemed really gross. Oh, I thought, for the first time: children are pregnant with themselves.

Unfortunately, once my appetite returned so did my flair for being judgmental.

Religious aspects of the baby

Her tossing and turning at night leadeth only to ascent, so that each morning she is head to the western border of the crib. Her pouring of sugar from cup to cup leadeth only to more sugar. When she unlinguines a box of linguine, then secrets away the pasta sticks into the bookshelves, within a zipper bag of pencils, under the pantry shelf, into a coat pocket, she revealeth the previously unconsidered negative spaces of the apartment. Her fear of the aloe plant at the neighbor's home is unmoved by the plant's persistently staying in place. Again and again she faces the challenge of the spoon, though its face turneth downwards and spilleth its contents, unless the contents of that spoon be yogurt, which hath imparted a false confidence, as it spilleth not, and in this way it deceiveth her, and yet even after repeated defeats with other-than-yogurt-substances, she returneth to the spoon with bright eyes and an open heart. When she desireth the opener of the cans, so as to turn the knob designed for arthritic hands with which she is happily acquainted, but the large person with whom she liveth denieth her the opener of the cans for the ancillary reason of the proximate rotating blade, she throws her head back and cries like a featherless bird.

Head shape

The puma was born with very little hair, giving all of us a clear view of the shape of her head. Or at least, giving a clear view of the shape of her head to anyone sensitive to head shape. What a beautifully shaped head she has! the baby's grandmother said, and then said again, and then said even yet again. Yes, I would say, in response to each head-shape compliment. But I felt uneasy: I had no idea what she was talking about. I had no sense at all of the shape of the baby's head. It seemed like a normal head. The baby's grandmother would then again say, What a beautifully shaped head, and I would again say, Yes, and then I would look even again at the baby's head—I would try to look dispassionately, in assessment—and would still not know what she was talking about. Yet the shape compliments kept coming in. One day, as if momentum had built up from the praise having been repeated so many times, it continued on into more detail: What a beautifully shaped head she has, it's so lovely … it's not at all like mine! And with that, the grandmother shook her own head slightly. I couldn't perceive then, and still fail to perceive now, anything particularly distinguished or undistinguished or even distinguishable about either of the referenced head shapes, but I accepted and continue to accept that the baby's grandmother must have been talking about something.

But what? I found myself relating this anecdote a number of times to a number of different people. I related the anecdote as if what interested me was the simple allegory of people noticing in babies whatever it is that preoccupies them about themselves. But that wasn't my real motive behind sharing the anecdote. The reason I kept telling the anecdote was that I was hoping to learn something about head shape. I kept waiting for someone to say, oh, yes, I know what she is talking about, and then to tell me. But no one was telling me. Then one evening I found myself at a dinner with a former supermodel. (The supermodel was writing a novel, her second, which is perhaps why she was at a small dinner with writers.) The baby was also there at the dinner. The baby's being there prompted the supermodel to say that she had never, never, never put her babies to sleep on their backs, that she knows that is what they do these days, but that she thinks it's a terrible idea because, for one, they could choke—that was what she was told by doctors, when her babies were young—and two, because putting babies to sleep on their backs means they end up with flat-backed heads. The former supermodel said that she didn't want to curse her babies with this problem, a problem that she herself had. A problem that she had long been embarrassed about, the weird flat-backed shape of her head. She demonstrated the back of her head. Which was, of course, like everything about her, beautiful. So I still didn't understand. I continued and continue to put the baby to bed on her back, though now that she is old enough to turn over, she shapes her own destiny.

The romantic comedy

My life with the very young human resembles those romantic comedies in which two people who don't speak
the same language still somehow fall in love. Like say, that
movie I saw on an airplane with the wide-eyed Brazilian
woman and the doofy American man who end up together, despite not being able to communicate via words.
Or that series of *Louie* episodes, where Louie falls in love
with a woman who only speaks Hungarian; he even pro-
poses to her. Yes, it was like those comedies, only without
the upsetting gender dynamic of the effectively mute female. Though with the same believability. And arguably
the dynamic might still be considered upsetting.

Wiped out

I used to sometimes find myself saying, "I'm wiped out."
After the puma was born I would very rarely, maybe
never, say I was "wiped out." Though I often thought to
myself, It's okay, I should just accept that I'm wiped out.
Maybe the puma had a cold, which disturbed her sleep,
and so it had been weeks since I had slept more than
an hour without interruption—there was always something, but also it was nothing, or, at times, I was nothing.
As the instances of thinking of myself as "wiped out"
accrued, I became sensitive to the phrase's hyperbolic
overlap with, say, a species being "wiped out." And also
to the fact that if at any given moment I introspected, I
was likely to discover that I felt "totally wiped out" and
so the sense of wiped out being a state that was relative
to some other non-wiped-out state had been lost; the
meaning of "wiped out" had been wiped out. The phrase
began to fade. Though I did, as if bartering, sometimes
find myself imagining a woman continually wiping dry
an irremediably damp table. Then one day recently I noticed I *wasn't* that wiped out, and I noticed this because I
saw that the puma had a dishtowel and she was using it
to wipe at water she had poured onto the floor.

The species

The baby loves to look at photos of babies. And at draw-ings of babies. And although she doesn't play with other babies often, she observes them on the street with an especial interest, with much more interest than she gives to a similarly aloof adult. Albeit with less attention than she would give to a dog. It's a very particular kind of in-terest, a mirror interest, I am guessing. She doesn't know yet that she is going to get bigger. She doesn't yet know that she will become one of us. We are of the large spe-cies; she is of the small species.

Literature has more dogs than babies

Literature has more dogs than babies, and also more abortions. Most babies who appear in literature are, by paragraph three, already children, if not even adults. But there are a few exceptions. In *Beloved* by Toni Morrison, a two-year-old baby is murdered by her mother so as to protect the child from a life of slavery, or from life at all, and the baby returns (it seems) as a ghost to haunt her family. A baby is an important character in Margaret Drabble's 1965 novel of a single mother in academia, *The Millstone*, albeit the baby appears more as a heavy pendant than as a being. And in Kenzaburo Oe's *A Personal Matter*, the narrator's baby is born with a seemingly deformed brain, extruded from his skull, and the narrator then travels around town with the baby, considers letting the baby die, but doesn't, considers sailing to Africa, but doesn't, and finally the narrator returns to the hospital and it turns out that the baby's deformity was only superficial and easily fixed, the baby is not a monster after all—so who *is* deformed? and who *is* a monster?—and the father, there in post–World War II Japan, is celebrated by his in-laws as if the good fortune is a reflection of his good moral character just as earlier his bad fortune was seen to be a reflection of his bad moral character. The novel *The Fifth Child* by Doris Lessing tells of a family with four children, and the whole family is pretty happy and ideal, even smug, until the catastrophically devilish fifth child is born, who, even as a baby, is terrifying. (Although one begins to notice that nobody other than his family seems to find the fifth child so difficult, or strange, and really the child seems simply not loved, and his only real fault as he grows up seems to be that he is more at ease in a class lower than that of the posh family who can no longer really afford the fantasy of the great house they inhabit.) In some of Lydia Davis's short stories, a baby often interrupts a thought, or is a thought. In Raymond Carver's "Feathers," a couple goes over for dinner to the house of another couple they don't know well, the house is a mess, there's a peacock wandering around, indoors, and then the visitors meet the host couple's baby, a baby about which the couple seem beatifically proud, and a baby who to the narrator is just enormously fat, the ugliest baby he has ever seen; and after witnessing the parents' love for their ugly baby, that same night the narrator and his wife go home and decide to have a baby themselves, and in the very end of the story we speed forward in time and find out that the man is upset that his wife cut her hair short and his life feels, with the baby, pressed and plain. In *Anna Karenina*, Tolstoy makes vivid and real both Anna's and Kitty's babies. (Tolstoy has also written about the inner life of a dying tree.) In Judy Budnitz's short-story collection *Nice Big American Baby*, several of the stories feature babies: one gestated for four years; another dark black though his parents are pale; many, many made by soldiers who are there and then gone. Maybe the most fully realized baby I have ever read appears in the Lorrie Moore story "People Like that Are the Only People Here," in which the baby is Baby and the father is Husband and the mother is Mother and the oncologist is Oncologist. In Jenny Offill's *Department of Speculation* we find a colicky and cherished baby and a breakdown (at least for a bit) of a marriage. I can think of no baby in Shakespeare, unless we count Caliban, which maybe we should. One might say that most babies in literature, when they appear for more than a moment, tend to be catalysts of decay or despair, as surely babies now and again in real life actually are (though literature is always only a convex looking glass, and not even a regularly convex one, more like an especially old and unshined spoon (and definitely a silver one)). So many of the modern written babies seem to have more in common with what are termed in Margaret Atwood's *A Handmaid's Tale* "unbabies" rather than "keepers." In their monstrous burdensomeness, these babies resemble my very favorite of all depicted babies, that nineteenth-century creature denied even the luxury of an infancy, that poor solitary wretch who on the first day of his life was already over six feet tall, and about whom his creator said, as if in repentance, "The world was to me a secret which I desired to divine." We're not to know. Mary Shelley's *Frankenstein* is not the infant joy of Coleridge or Blake, instead it is the story of an infant angry about being born at all, a half-rhyme emotionally with the book itself being termed by its mother/author to be her "hideous progeny"—a phrase more sad than flip, as Mary Shelley knew herself to be the progeny whose arrival led to the death of her mother, Mary Wollstonecraft, the vindicator of the rights of women. (And Mary Shelley then had to watch, after writing her book, her first, second, and third child die in infancy.) But if I seem to be wandering into an appraisal of babies—so underrepresented!—as in need of their own subaltern studies then I have wandered too far. We know babies are the only ones among us in alliance with time. They are the only incontestable accessors to power, or, at least, they are immeasurably more well-placed than their elder co-unequals. The way a baby, in a stroller, briefly resembles a fat potentate, for a moment unlovable, has something in it of the premonition. Even as to see a baby raise its chubby hand—to bow down before that random emperor can feel very right.

More Frankenstein

Frankenstein isn't the name of the monster, it is only the name of the creator of the monster, and the monster himself is never given a name, which contributes to the productive confusion that leads most people, even those who know better, to think of and speak of the creature as "Frankenstein."

Dr. Frankenstein, the father (and mother) in a sense, notices the creature, shortly after creation, peering over the edge of a bed, like a toddler in his parents' room. Dr. Frankenstein flees in terror from the sight. The creature is then left on his own. For awhile he hangs out around the house of a family he dreams of belonging to; the head of that family is a blind man; the creature one day gathers the courage to present himself to the kind, blind man; the man listens, sensitively, to the creature's story; then the man's children return, scream in terror, and fight the "monster" off, even as said monster cries and clings to the knees of the blind father, as would a very young child.

After that, the creature becomes angry, and violent—also like a young child.

The creature eats only fruits and berries, and never meat.

Most people report that when seeing babies they have a desire to eat them.

So babies do appear in literature maybe more than we might first notice.

And movies

Among the things commonly noted about the original *Godzilla* movie is that it came out in 1954 and was the first movie to acknowledge the bombing of Hiroshima and Nagasaki, though it acknowledges it obliquely. Godzilla is said to have been awoken by nuclear testing, his footprints are radioactive, and the only English words in the movie are *Geiger counter* and *oxygen destroyer*. Also a woman on a commuter train says, of Godzilla, "First the acid rain, and now Godzilla."

But Godzilla doesn't necessarily mean to do harm; malice isn't a fundamental aspect of his character. In a sense he has no malice at all, only rage. My favorite scene in *Godzilla* is the brief one in which we see Godzilla underwater, in his (or maybe her) natural setting. Underwater Godzilla is played by an obviously small toy. The toy is a much less detailed special-effects creature than aboveground Godzilla. Underwater Godzilla seahorses around on the ocean floor as extra-diegetic classical music plays; his gentle pulsing movements almost make it seem as if the underwater Godzilla has himself put the delicate music on, on an unseen underwater stereo. These "bad" special effects contribute, perfectly, to the overall effect: Godzilla is a childlike creature, innocent of his destructions. Even aboveground Godzilla walks widely, like a toddler. I read once of studies looking into the question of when it was that violent criminals became violent; the studies concluded that it wasn't that violence suddenly appeared, it was that in some people more than others, for whatever reasons, the natural violence of youth was never extinguished.

Princess Kaguya

The baby seems younger today, her hand reaching out, grasping and ungrasping like a sea anemone. I pick up something I have read before, something especially short; I have the baby bound and burritoed in a thin blanket next to me, I position her on her side, so she can stare at the black-and-white notecards slotted between the sofa cushions, and she seems content, and I read the story again; the story, *The Tale of the Bamboo Cutter*, is based on a Japanese myth at least 1,200 years old.

The tale tells of an elderly bamboo cutter who one day comes across a glowing stalk of bamboo. Inside the stalk, he finds a tiny, tiny baby girl. He brings the girl home and he and his wife raise her as their own. The previously poor and childless couple now find gold each time they go out to cut more bamboo. The girl grows quickly into the most beautiful girl in the land, drawing the notice even of the Emperor. But the girl is moody. She has no interest in suitors. She spends a lot of time looking at the night sky. One day, a spaceship arrives; it turns out the girl is from another planet! The gold in the bamboo was a gift in thanks to her adoptive parents for keeping her safe; there had been war on her planet, but now it was time for her to return to where she truly belonged. The girl boards the spaceship and leaves, forever.

Suddenly the strange old myth seems to be just a straightforward and basically realistic tale about babies: their arrival feels supernatural, they seem to come from another world, life near them takes on a certain unaccountable richness, and they are certain, eventually, to leave you. A more "realistic" description of a baby—e.g., "born after a seventeen-hour labor … at 7 pounds 11 ounces … nursing every two hours … smiling at eight weeks, grasping at twelve weeks …"—misses most everything. Only the supernatural gets at the actual. Or so it can seem to a mother on a good day, at least to the mother of a relatively easy baby, who is lying on her side, looking at a picture of an owl.

Rumpelstiltskin

Rumpelstiltskin is a small man with the exuberance and temper of a two-year-old child. He helps the miller's daughter spin straw into gold. He helps her in this way not once, not twice, but three times! His help saves both the miller's daughter and the miller. In some versions of the story, this even leads to the miller's daughter's marriage to the king. But Rumpelstiltskin doesn't do this for nothing; the third time he spins straw into gold, he does so in exchange for the miller's daughter's future as yet unconceived firstborn.

Still, Rumpelstiltskin isn't too bad a guy. When the miller's daughter doesn't want to hand over her firstborn, Rumpelstiltskin offers her an out. He doesn't have to offer her an out, but he does. That's why he's kind of sweet. The famous out that he offers her—if she can guess his name within three tries then she doesn't have to give over her baby—wasn't part of their original deal. Why does he offer her an out at all?

Maybe naming a newborn baby isn't all that different from guessing the name of Rumpelstiltskin: any name is possible, but only one name proves to be right. It almost seems as if what Rumpelstiltskin is trying to do is to get the miller's daughter to remember that she is his mother. Rumpelstiltskin's name, in all the versions, in all the languages, translates into something like, "dear little goblin who makes noise with a stilt." *He* is the firstborn, *he* is the original source of gold; he's ambivalent about having a sibling.

How the puma affects others, one

A friend has two children with a woman to whom he
is no longer married and he is now with a woman who
has no children, and who probably wants to have children, though none of this has been openly discussed
with me, I am surmising. The two children of the friend
are now teenagers, and they themselves have a half sibling already, from their mother's side, their mother who
is known to be appealing but unreliable, able to land,
say, in Chicago, before beginning to make phone calls
to arrange for babysitting for her children in New York.
My friend pays the half sibling's college expenses. One
gets the sense that he fears raising children again with
someone who may reveal themselves to be not necessarily internally outfitted in a way suitable for the care of
children, but again all of this is surmising, and my friend
never mentions thoughts about maybe, or maybe not,
having another baby, and knowing him as I do, it is reasonable to guess that he has also maybe not mentioned
these thoughts to himself.

One evening, this friend arrives at our home, to meet
the puma, when she is fresh, less than two weeks old. He

arrives wearing a forty-pound vest. The vest, he says, is recommended as a way to build strength and endurance. It's just a thing he's trying out. He just now walked the ten blocks from his home to our home, not too far. But with the vest. His teenage children and his girlfriend are with him too. They are often with him. He is very close to all of them. They say nothing about the vest. He apologizes for being a little late. He had been in a class for potential foster parents, he explains. We have never heard anything about this fostering interest before; it is new. "You always dream of just the normal kid, with no issues, who's been orphaned by a car crash," he said explaining his hesitation, but interest, in taking on foster children. "But apparently it's much more difficult than that."

How the puma affects others, two

We live at the intersection of Penn Station, the Port Authority, and the Lincoln Tunnel. Very few babies make their home in this area, while a relatively high number of men without homes make their homes here. Between the front door of our building and the butcher shop at the corner there lives a very slim Hispanic man who sometimes sweeps the sidewalk, and who sometimes helps the catering company next door move their boxes, and who sometimes just stands around. Once I saw him directing buses out of the nearby bus parking lot. He is sometimes well, and smoking a cigarette and making conversation with the catering and food cart and garment guys on the block, and he is at other times not well, and half-asleep on the sidewalk. When I first moved to the neighborhood, one afternoon when I walked by him, and he was sitting on the sidewalk, leaning against the wall of the butcher shop, he spat on me and shouted, "Ugly!" After he spat on me a second time, I took to crossing the street to avoid him, especially when I was pregnant, and generally more cautious than usual.

But in those first couple months at home with the puma, the environment around me blurred, like in those photos taken with the f-stop set just so, and one day I didn't notice this man who lives on our block, and so I didn't cross the street to avoid him, I instead walked right by him, and I heard someone shouting at me—it was him shouting at me—"God bless you! What a beautiful baby boy. Take care of that boy." This has consistently been his response to our passing ever since. Even though the puma now occasionally wears a dress. Now, when we walk by, he and the little girl invariably exchange a high five. But not really invariably. When he is smoking, he suggests that she not come too near.

Notes on some twentieth-century writers

Flannery O'Connor: No children.

Eudora Welty: No children. One children's book.

Hilary Mantel, Janet Frame, Willa Cather, Jane Bowles,
Patricia Highsmith, Elizabeth Bishop, Hannah Arendt,
Iris Murdoch, Djuna Barnes, Gertrude Stein, Virginia
Woolf, Katherine Mansfield, Mavis Gallant, Simone de
Beauvoir, Barbara Pym: No children.

Helen Gurley Brown, author of *Having It All*: no children.

Katherine Anne Porter: No children, many husbands.

Alice Munro: Three children. Two husbands. First story
collection at age thirty-seven.

Toni Morrison: Two children. First novel at age thirty-
nine.

Penelope Fitzgerald: Three children. First novel age sixty.
Then eight more novels.

John Updike: Many children. Many books. First book
age twenty-five.

Saul Bellow: Many children. Many wives. Many books.
First at age twenty-nine.

Doris Lessing: Left two of her three children to be raised
by her father. Later semiadopted a teenage girl, a peer

of one of her sons. Said, and had to repeatedly handle questions about having said, that there was "nothing more boring for an intelligent woman than to spend endless amounts of time with small children." Many books.

Muriel Spark: One child, born in Southern Rhodesia during her marriage to Sydney Oswald Spark, who suffered from manic depression. She moved to London alone, leaving behind her husband. Her young son, also left behind, ended up in the care of some fruit sellers down the road, before he eventually moved to Scotland to live with his maternal grandparents. The child was later disinherited by his mother, who was annoyed, it is said, that he went around complaining that his mother wouldn't admit that she was Jewish. Among other things. Many books.

Rebecca West: Had one child with H. G. Wells, to whom she was not married. Tried to convince the child that she was his aunt and not his mother (arguably for his own good). In 1955, the child wrote a roman à clef, *Heritage*, about the son of two world-famous parents; the mother does not come off well. For twenty-nine years, West successfully blocked publication. In 1984, when the novel was finally released, the child, aged sixty-nine, wrote an introduction to the book that further condemned his mother. The same year, the child published a laudatory biography of his mostly absent father.

Shirley Jackson: Four children.

J. G. Ballard: Widowed with three young children. Drank every day, was very productive, and called all of his children, in his autobiography of the same name, "miracles of life." In describing seeing his children newly born, he wrote, "Far from being young, as young as a human being can be, they seemed immensely old, their foreheads and features streamlined by time, as archaic and smooth as the heads of pharaohs in Egyptian sculpture, as if they had traveled an immense distance to find their parents. Then, in a second, they became young." Ballard also wrote with fondness about his time as a child in the internment camps of Shanghai.

Other people's babies

Are often noted to not be of interest.

Other people's babies, two

Every hour, about 14,500 babies are born.

Other people's babies, three

When Lucille Ball was pregnant, her character on television was also pregnant, though the word pregnant, like a swear word, could not, at the time, be said on television; Lucy was, instead, expecting. She carried bags, and stood behind chairs and sofas, so as to protect viewers from a full visual sense of what was expected. Lucille's husband on the show, Ricky Ricardo, was played by her actual husband, Desi Arnaz. In real life, Lucille Ball turned down show-business offers until someone was willing to also employ Desi Arnaz, who, probably because he was Cuban, was mostly denied employment. This dynamic is reversed in *I Love Lucy*. Ricky Ricardo is a successful bandleader at a nightclub, and a regular plot point is Lucy's desperate attempts to be part of his show. The episode of *I Love Lucy* in which Little Ricky is born was watched by forty-four million Americans, in three out of every four homes that had a television, and was titled, simply, *Lucy Goes to the Hospital*.

Other people's babies, four

For the first photos of the twins of Brad Pitt and Angelina Jolie, *People* paid fourteen million dollars.

Reversals

Murasaki Shikibu, of *The Tale of Genji*, and Sei Shonagon, of *The Pillow Book*, knew one another. They weren't fond of one another. Shikibu was reserved and retiring, and more well-placed politically; Shonagon was witty and conversationally brilliant, and had a less stable position at court. Tutored by their fathers, both women knew Chinese, which was then the language of power and of politics (and of serious literature), and it was a language that women were not taught; women were supposed to speak and write only in Japanese; both women wrote their masterworks in Japanese, the insignificant language of women and gossip.

After *The Pillow Book* and *The Tale of Genji*, the third most noted and enduring book from the Heian period is *The Tosa Nikki*. It is a sort of travelogue, written in Japanese, by a male author writing under a female pseudonym, and its opening line is, "I hear that diaries are things that men make but let's see what a woman can do."

Mother writers

Both Murasaki Shikibu and Sei Shonagon had, it seems, babies. I don't know to what extent ladies at Heian court raised their babies. From the books it is difficult to tell. But at least, it would appear, somewhat. Even empresses nursed. Shikibu in her diaries describes the patheticness of her empress's baby not quite latching on. Shonagon complains in *The Pillow Book* of overly possessive wet nurses. Shonagon's empress, a different empress than Shikibu's, is sent away from court to have her baby, and though it was normal to be sent away, she was sent somewhere conspicuously low in status, she's in political decline, and the passage in which Shonagon describes this pregnant exile is one of the most willfully cheerful passages in the whole book; that empress dies shortly after giving birth.

Today there are many writers who are mothers, sometimes writing specifically about motherhood, and in a genre that we recognize as literature. Or, at least, there are some mother writers, in this sense, if not many. There is Elena Ferrante, and Sarah Manguso. But among the mother writers of today probably two of the most celebrated are men: Karl Ove Knausgaard and, in his way, Louis C. K.

When the baby came home

I set her down in her crib, and she didn't cry. Why, I wondered, is she not distressed? It's as if she assumes that we will, of course, love and care for her. It seemed so strange for her to assume that. I respected her fearlessness.

When the empress moved

The passage in *The Pillow Book* titled "When the Empress Moved" tells of all the amusing and comic things that happen when the empress Teishi and her court (including Shonagon) are moved out of the main palace to another residence, one where the gate is not wide enough for the carriage to pass, where the master of the house doesn't know the words for things, and where the court ladies are not given their proper privacy. In this passage, Shonagon does not mention that the empress Teishi is pregnant and ill, that another woman from another family was also recently named empress, that the move to a house far beneath her station was a political one, part of an attempt to shift power to a different family, and she also does not mention that the empress Teishi will soon die in childbirth, an event that has most likely already happened when the passage was written but which isn't encompassed in the passage. Instead the writing is crowded over with laughter and "charm," and scholars tell us that the passage has a special density of what in Japanese aesthetics is known as *okashii*—the amusing and the strange—and this high incidence of *okashii* (as opposed to *aware*, roughly translated to us as the pathos of things passing) often increases in *The Pillow Book* at moments when we might expect the opposite, at moments of distress and loss. (This is part of what makes me associate the book with what I think of as the "small" as opposed to the "minor.")

Then the section that immediately *follows* that of "When the Empress Moved" (and though we can't be certain of the original order of the passages, it is plausible that they were in this order) is one full of the touchingly named quality of *aware*. It tells of a once-favored palace dog who is punished by being cast out from the palace—sent to Dog Island!—and who eventually makes his way back, injured and emaciated. The returned dog pretends to be a different dog, but cries telling tears when his true name is mentioned. Eventually, the dog receives an imperial pardon—his offense had been to startle a beloved cat who wore an imperial headdress and was known as Lady Myobu, that was why he was banished—and he is thereafter, according to Shonagon, "returned to his former happy state." She continues, "Yet even now, when I remember how he whimpered and trembled in response to our sympathy, it strikes me as a strange and moving scene; when people talk to me about it, I start crying myself." It is the passage with the happy ending that closes in tears.

The Pillow Book is difficult to characterize. It's not a novel and not a diary and not poems and not advice, but it has qualities of each, and it would have been understood at the time as a kind of miscellany, a familiar form. The book consists of 185 entries, many of them quite short, some of them anecdotes, some lists, some pronouncements. "Oxen should have very small foreheads with white hair," one short section begins. "A preacher ought to be good-looking," begins another, but the passage then bumps into, "But I really must stop writing this kind of thing. If I were still young enough, I might risk the consequence of putting down such impieties, but at my present stage of life I should be less flippant."

Often Shonagon seems wildly petty about issues of "taste"—"Nothing can be worse than allowing the driver of one's ox carriage to be poorly dressed"—and we have to remember that the writer of the passage, Shonagon, was a person whose very delimited power derived almost exclusively from her expert manipulation of the language of passing fashions. She knows the best way to starch cottons, what colors look best under what other colors, and just how to hold a fan; this arena of tiny decisions was a kind of politics, and the only kind available to her. In her list, "Things that have lost their power," we find

> a woman who has taken off her false locks to comb the short hair that remains ... A large tree that has been blown down in a gale and lies on its side with its roots in the air ... The retreating figure of a sumo wrestler who has been defeated in a match ... A woman who is angry with her husband about some trifling matter, leaves home and goes somewhere to hide. She is certain that he will rush about looking for her; but he does nothing of the kind and shows the most infuriating indifference. Since she cannot stay away for ever, she swallows her pride and returns.

Scholars are not even sure of what Shonagon's real name was, but it is known that her father was a poet, that she was not considered naturally beautiful, and that whether she died an impoverished nun in the countryside or in mild gentility with a second husband is not clear.

My very favorite entry in *The Pillow Book* is a not-so-simple story Shonagon tells about "the woman's hand." "The woman's hand" is written in Japanese, rather than Chinese. The passage begins simply:

> The Captain First Secretary, Tadanobu, having heard certain false rumors, began to speak about me in the most

unpleasant terms. "How could I have thought of her as a human being?" was the sort of thing he used to say …

Not mentioned in the passage is that Tadanobu was formerly Shonagon's lover, and he had recently been promoted to a high position in court. His new hatred of Shonagon is not just emotionally painful, but also a threat; Shonagon, like any court lady, was always at risk of being sent away from court, as soon as her presence was no longer considered charming, but this possibility is not emphasized in the telling; instead Shonagon tries to laugh off the problem. She then hears word that Tadanobu has admitted that life has "after all been a bit boring without" Shonagon. Shortly after, a messenger arrives for Shonagon with a letter from Tadanobu. She doesn't want to be flustered when she reads it, so she tells the messenger to leave and that she'll send a reply later; the messenger says no, that his master told him that if he didn't get a reply right away he should take the letter back. Shonagon opens the letter, and finds the opening stanza of a Chinese poem:

> With you it is flower time
> As you sit in the Council Hall
> 'Neath a curtain of brocade.

Beneath the verse, the powerful former lover has added: How does the stanza end?

The poem is one written by a revered poet, Po Chu-I, while he was in exile. Sending a Chinese poem to a woman should make no sense—a woman wasn't supposed to know Chinese, the language of politics and high poetry. (*The Pillow Book* is written in Japanese, the common language.) Tadanobu has set a sort of trap for Shonagon. For her to demonstrate her knowledge of Chinese would be unfeminine. Either she can appear to be ignorant—and Tadanobu knows she takes pride in her intelligence—or she can respond, knowingly, in Chinese, which would reveal her at once to have a weak Chinese script and also to being vulgarly open about the fact that she was versed in Chinese at all.

Shonagon takes a piece of charcoal from the fire and uses it to write, in Japanese, in "the woman's hand," at the bottom of Tadanobu's note:

> Who would come to visit
> This grass-thatched hut of mine?

The words are the closing lines from another poem written by another poet, also in exile, but it is a poem written in Japanese. In contrast to the Council Hall and brocade, the grass-thatched hut is a humble setting; Japanese, as opposed to Chinese, is the humble language;

the charcoal is more humble than ink; the question is a more submissive form than the statement; the addressee shows herself to be none of the things the addresser suggests in the initial stanza, in fact the opposite; but the display of wit and learning, at once veiled and visible, is a display of the one kind of power Shonagon has; knowing how to obscure that power passably, in an elegant humility—is its own further show of virtuosity. Also the note, in content, is a simple invitation of love.

"How can one break from a woman like that?" a friend says to Tadanobu.

Within a day, all of the Emperor's gentlemen have Shonagon's response written on their fans. Shonagon becomes not only the confection of choice, but also a kind of legend at court. For her small witticism, her tiny act. But it's along a web of such small elegances that Shonagon survives, since she is not beautiful, and not noble, and soon enough not young either. Every week she is more at risk of being sent away, and even her own intelligence, which is what saves her, also makes her vulnerable. She can't stand the sight of her reflection, or the sight of other women in decline, and that revulsion also fuels her work. "I cannot stand a woman who wears sleeves of unequal width," she says. And "When I make myself imagine what it is like to be one of those women who live at home … I am filled with scorn." As a samurai's judgment of a ronin makes psychological sense as someone catching sight of themselves in a lower state, Shonagon is never more rough than on figures who resemble her. In her list of "unsuitable things" she notes: "A woman who is well past her youth is pregnant and walks along panting." Another passage describes a visit from a beggar nun who is asking for offerings from the altar—asking, basically, for food. Shonagon and the other court women are amused by the beggar nun, who dances and sings, but they are also repelled by her clothing and manners, which are repeatedly described as disgusting. The ladies prepare a package of food for the beggar nun, and then complain that she keeps coming around; we hear that the beggar's voice is curiously refined; the fate of the beggar nun could easily be that of the women then at court, though this is never said. Instead, the beggar nun passage switches abruptly into a lengthy anecdote about all sorts of hopes and bets among the court ladies as to which mound of snow made in the castle courtyard will last the longest; none of the court ladies wins;

Shonagon prepares a poem about the last of the snow; the empress has the snow swept away, ruining the game; Shonagon is more devastated by this than seems to make sense; but the empress has treated her court ladies in the same indulgent then indifferent way that the court ladies treated the beggar nun; Shonagon juxtaposes the scenes so that we see each person, even the empress, slipping in power, clinging to the tiny entertainments they can offer, their only currency. Taste culture helplessly tells another story.

Screens

The resolution is that the baby will have no relationship to screens—no iPhones, no iPads, no televisions, none of whatever it is that's out there. "You have to get her a video machine," my mother said, referring to her understanding of what technology might be out there. "You need to get her some programming, maybe in French," my brother said. When I was young there was a desperate imperative to get computers into schools. Nowadays I read of studies that show that laptops given to children in rural African villages have ruined students' education, the kids' grades fall, the kids drop out. Another day I read that children who have a lot of "screen time" experience schematic diagrams of corners differently than children with little or no screen time. The implications of alternative ways of understanding diagrams of corners is obscure to me, but it seems important nevertheless. Maybe even paramount. I also read that children who cease to use screens for a time as short as one week make more eye contact and score better on tests of reading emotions on the faces of others. Sure, "studies" is usually just another word for mildly evidenced nonsense, but there they are. I myself spent eight or nine hours a day as a child watching television, mostly reruns of sitcoms. Though I am not a completely empty soul, I do feel that I could be improved upon. My child will not have screens, I decide. Not for a long time. Yet somehow, by the time she is one year old, my daughter can play music, page through photos, and call long distance on my iObject. This development happens off-screen.

iPhone footage

iPhone footage of the puma has the unfortunate quality of making it seem as if the puma has passed away and the watcher, me, is condemned to replaying the same scene again and again and again. The more banal the scene, the more intense this effect. Footage of her crawling across a room to pick up a toy skateboard and then eat a piece of strawberry—a heartrending seven-second loop. I imagine this has to do with some sort of intensified sensation of time passing, brought about by being in touch with the illusion of time standing still. Or with boredom, or hostility, or love. But I discover that the affective qualities of loops are different for the puma. When she watches the same footage again and again and again she looks like someone who has been given access to a holy book and is not afraid of the messages it bears.

Lots of writers have children

Sometimes those children write memoirs. It is rare that the memoirs are happy memoirs. This may say more about the nature of memoirs than the nature of being the child of a writer. (Whether being the child of a writer is really any worse than being the child of an accountant professor grocer realtor regulator will remain difficult to say since selection bias—children of writers more likely to write—makes memoirs, in relation to this question, a more than usually problematic dataset.) There is a certain consistency of complaint, I have noticed, among these memoirs: the child comes to show something to the writer-parent, who is writing in a room at home during the daytime hours, and the writer-parent says to the child, I can't right now, I'm working. There are also often descriptions of the looming, hostile, uncompromising door of the home office. Apparently it is very troubling for children to see their parents working, at least doing the kind of work that does not make itself visibly obvious, even if the total hours of work, and thus parental unavailability, are

73

equal (or more likely substantially less) than the working hours of a parent simply leaving the house, to go, say, to an office, where the equally mysterious work of "office work" is, in the child's imagination, if they are interested in the imagining, done. Presumably these doors are simply the wrong doors on which to be knocking. I have consistently had a difficult time believing these memoirs, not that one has to believe memoirs, or that belief is what memoirs are there for. But the door seems like an obvious screen door. But screen for what?

I have never been the child of a writer, nor been a writer who had a child. (Being a writer who has a baby is really nothing like being a writer who has a child.) But I was once taking care of a three-year-old child, my niece, while I had no choice but to, in at least a minimal way, be working as a writer at the same time. It was the first time I was having a story of mine published in a major magazine, and I had to go over edits on the phone at a specific time, a time which overlapped with my picking up my niece from her preschool and then passing a couple hours with her, in a nearby Starbucks, until her parents were home—I didn't have a key to their apartment. My niece was and is an unusually easy, flexible child. I took her to the designated Starbucks, though the original reason for going to the Starbucks, which was Internet access (this was more than a decade ago), proved dysfunctional that afternoon. Regardless, I opened my laptop and tried to take the editorial call. It was a call, then calls back, it was going back and forth. My niece was annoyed that I wasn't speaking only to her. I promised I would speak with her soon. I continued to speak on the phone, with the editor. At one point, in between phone calls, my niece told me she wanted to go to the bathroom, so I brought her to the bathroom. Once were in the narrow stall, she took my phone from my coat pocket and threw it in the toilet. The phone did not work after that.

It is nice for children when their parents have offices outside of the home and are not seen to be doing work, I note to myself today, as the puma weeps while I speak on the cellphone, briefly, for work.

In Flagstaff, one

I am outside with the young chicken, in front of our conspicuously nice rental in Flagstaff, Arizona. The rental is an assemblage of shipping containers, insulated by a special ecologically sound paint, and oriented just so to the sun, etc., and on the sidewalk in the distance, I see a woman approaching with her two young daughters, who are dressed beautifully. There's also a man, a few paces behind her, carrying an open cardboard box of canned and boxed goods. The man waves, somehow too soon, from too far away, and too familiarly. It's weird. It makes him seem drunk or high. I wave back. A short time later, the woman waves too, as do the children, who, as they near, approach the young chicken with interest; the young chicken is shy with them. The older girl kneels down to be on a level with the young chicken; she asks her mother if she can give the little girl one of her gummy bears; the mother tells me that the gummy bears are organic; the chicken doesn't take the gummy bear, and the mother tells her daughters not to worry about it, that not everyone likes gummy bears. The girls are Kaysia and Shalia, the mother says, they are three and seven. The man is standing a few feet off, grinning widely. The mother asks me if I live around here and I say that I don't, and then I ask her if she lives around here and she says that it's complicated. The children, along with the chicken, have wandered about ten feet away, to the driveway of our rental, and their mother is explaining to me that although she was born in Pennsylvania, she was kidnapped by her mom when she was eleven months old, after which they lived in Canada, in Mexico, eventually in Los Angeles, until, when she was three and a half years old, the authorities caught up with them. "My brother thought my dad was a ghost," she tells me, laughing. Then they returned to Pennsylvania, lived with their dad. Her mother was in jail in Pennsylvania, so they could visit her. I didn't know what to say. I asked the woman, How were things now with her parents, did she get along with them? She said that in the past year her dad had died, and that her mom is in Phoenix, dying of cancer, she is taking care of her, it has been a difficult year; she said that the father of her youngest was suing her for $10,000 in court, and she couldn't afford that, she is still a university student, studying to be a math teacher, she loves math, always has, she lives in Phoenix now, not here, she is just in Flagstaff to visit her old friend, Ray; at this, she gestured to the man with the box who was still standing a few feet away. He was still grinning, and he still didn't approach. The mother is an unusually pretty woman. Somehow we are still standing there, together. The chemical equation between us seems to be off, as if atoms are going to shift from one side to the other, because that is the law. It has to balance out. She's still chatting and chatting. Then I hear my daughter crying. She is lying on her back on the pavement of the driveway. The two young girls are looking at their mother, and at me. The older girl says, We were trying to help her stand up again and that was when she fell over.

In Flagstaff, two

The oviraptor is one of the small Mongolian theropod dinosaurs. Its name means, more or less, "egg thief." It turns out this name is unfair. The first oviraptor fossil was discovered near a nest, which is how the name came about. But years later it was decided that the oviraptor was most likely near its own nest when it died, that the eggs in the nest were most likely its own eggs.

I learn this from a label on a model of the original oviraptor fossil at a gift shop labeled Museum Gift Shop Information, located just outside of the Petrified National Forest. The gift shop has stones, fossils, mugs, moccasins, key chains, polished quartz, unpolished quartz, Navajo-style blankets for $10, and Navajo-style blankets for $400—it is about 4,000 square feet of floorspace organized like the attic of a nostalgic geologist. We are the only customers there on a bright, clear day. There are two people working there, a very thin woman wearing a thick blonde wig, and a young man who appears to be her son and who inspects my driver's license to coordinate it with my credit card for a very long time; though we came in for a map, we are buying a toddler-sized pair of red moccasins. When we ask how long the drive is through the Petrified Forest and the Painted Desert, the thin woman says that we shouldn't miss the information booth, the official one, which is just inside the park. She says, So many people think that *this* is the information booth, because we have the word Information on our roof, but the information booth is just further in, and there you can find a map.

New variety of depression

It's true what they say, that a baby gives you a reason to live. But also, a baby is a reason that it is not permissible to die. There are days when this does not feel good.

A *baby is an ideal vector for a revenge plot*

In some sense, *The Tale of Genji* has no plot. Genji is born, then this happens and that happens and then he gets old and he dies and other people continue on, living their lives, in which further thises and thats happen.

But in another sense Genji has a perfectly rounded plot: it describes a simple triptych with the unavoidable ambiguity of paternity as its hinges. Genji is born to the most beloved of the emperor's consorts, but she dies shortly after Genji is born; because she was of low status, her son Genji is also of problematically low status. But the emperor then marries a woman who looks like Genji's deceased mother, and later Genji has an affair with that stepmother, and he and the stepmother then pretend that the resultant child is the emperor's. That child eventually becomes emperor. As emperor he grants status to Genji, his real father. Genji, by this time, has gone on to marry a woman he met when she was a young girl and whom he raised as if she were his daughter. Later Genji's third wife has a child with Genji's evil nephew and *they* pretend *that* child is Genji's. That child, who becomes a basically mediocre and evil man, lives on after Genji's death with the status of a son of Genji.

So twice major characters fall in love with people who are essentially, if not biologically, their children. And twice the ambiguity of paternity enables a radical shift of power: once it elevates Genji, via his secret son, and once it diminishes Genji, via his secretly not-son. That first shift is a revenge against inheritance, the second shift is a revenge upon that revenge. It is a wise child that knows its own father, goes the saying. And a wise mother who makes use of the mystery. The novel ends in midsentence, and no one really knows if the final words are those of Lady Murasaki, or if the last chapters were written not by Murasaki herself but instead, after her death, by her daughter.

A *modern anxiety*

Paternal ambiguity is age-old. Maternal ambiguity is pretty new. Of course babies could be switched, and stories of changelings were useful ways of understanding strange children, but still, carrying a child in one's body meant that even the most magical thoughts were alloyed with maternal certainty. In vitro fertilization has altered this.

Or, at least, I found myself, starting when the baby was about eleven days old, and then for months afterward, thinking in detail through the following problem: If it turned out I had carried someone else's child, what should I do? (The doctor had seemed a hasty, careless type.) What would constitute ethical behavior? Would it be wrong to flee the country with the baby, in order to stay together? We were already so in love—wasn't love its own validity? If I gave the baby over to her "real" mother, was I allowed to stay in touch, or was I required to let her go entirely? It was so obvious what the right thing to do was, and so obvious, also, that I would not do it. This was distressing even though I also knew that I would never be so called upon.

One could argue that this is a straightforward prefig-uration of the difficulties of allowing a child to grow up and away. Or that it's evidence that even with insufficient sleep and no free time, a certain kind of mind will find its way toward an excess of immaterial quandaries. Or maybe I was just working through my problematic in-ability to hand the child over to another caretaker, even for just a few hours.

Things that one was misleadingly told were a big part of having a baby

Diapers. Changing them. Bottles. Cleaning them. Wraps. Baths. Sleeplessness. Cheerios. All these things exist, but rise to consciousness about as often as the apartment's electricity does.

Babies in art

Babies in art mostly look nothing like babies in life. This is especially true of the baby Jesus, but also of babies more broadly, and this is true even, and maybe most noticeably, in paintings and sculptures that are, apart from the oddly depicted babies, realistic. Often babies are depicted with the proportions of small adults: their limbs are relatively longer than baby limbs, and their heads are not as relatively large as baby heads; in real life babies have heads so large, and arms so short, that they can't reach their arms beyond their heads. But one almost never sees this in a museum. I am told, also, that a major problem through the centuries for artists depicting the baby Jesus has been the question of what to do about the Lord's penis.

Recently, though, the baby and I saw several realistic paintings of babies. One of these was by the seventeenth-century artist Jan Steen, who is most famous for his paintings of chaotic, messy households—households as they really were, one imagines. Also we saw a Jan de Bray painting titled *The Adoration of the Shepherds*, which depicted the infant Jesus looking like a real infant; *Adoration* was hung near *Still Life with Strawberries* by Adriaen Coorte. All the paintings were in the same room, which had, as the focal point of the gallery, a very large painting of a cow, by Paulus Potter. It had been radical at the time, the gallery copy noted, for a simple cow to be the subject of such attentive portraiture.

So there was a moment, in Dutch painting, when the problem of how to depict babies was solved by having them appear as they in fact are. But I think I've discovered a more pervasive and enduring realistic depiction of babies, though not in depictions of actual babies but instead in depictions of the virgin Mary. I had often wondered about the distinctive tilt of Mary's head in so many paintings and sculptures. It's a very particular, recognizable tilt, and you see it again and again, across time and geography. The tilt is usually coincident with Mary holding but not necessarily looking at the baby Jesus. In iconography, I imagine, the tilt has its own prescribed meaning. But that's an insufficient explanation of the tilt, of why it came to be, of why it makes sense. It's not a tilt I've ever observed in women in real life. But after I held my young baby again and again and again and again and again, I very clearly recognized the angle of the tilt of Mary's head; it is the tilt of the head of babies who are just beginning to develop the strength of their neck muscles. When I hold my baby, she holds her head at that exact same angle.

Video games

You love to touch metal, running over subway gratings, sidewalk cellar doors, manhole covers ... you get very frustrated if you are denied the chance to run over these metals. I now understand Donkey Kong.

Orange

When the puma was about four months old, exiting the feline state and just beginning to move toward the sloth state, it was regularly cold enough outside that she traveled nearly everywhere in a bright-orange full-body puffy snowsuit. She looked especially helpless and magnificent in it. The snowsuit had been a gift, purchased for her from an online company devoted to baby things; the company's website also had, as its main marketing color, the same orange, a variety one might describe as safety orange, or avalanche-gear orange. Most objects on the website were available in pink, blue, and then also orange, or, sometimes, only orange.

Meanwhile, the snowsuit. On an elevator, a woman joked that she wanted to trade outfits with the baby. At a meeting with an editor, the editor said of the snowsuit: What brand is that, do they also make coats for adults? The coat elicited positive comments at a rate commensurate with that of positive comments about the baby herself, who had just begun to smile. Actually, in truth, there were more comments about the coat than about the baby. I myself found the coat/snowsuit magically beautiful too, I confess, even as I don't particularly love the color orange, but somehow in the case of the coat/snowsuit, it was the orangeness specifically that was compelling. It felt talismanic. How it comes to be that one year we are drawn to safety orange, another year to emerald green, another to heather gray, is inevitably difficult to untangle. But occasionally the influence can be persuasively traced: for example the brief emerald trend of a few years back I attribute specifically to a run of emerald Cornell t-shirts that said, in contrasting white, *Ithaca is Gorges*; they glittered briefly across the city; other emerald-colored items followed; then the green disappeared. The brief return, one spring, of skirts shorter in the front than in the back followed the release of a Diane Keaton memoir which included a photo of her in such a skirt; that old-fashioned cut of skirt returned for a few months and then, like a desert bloom, was again gone and likely won't be seen again for decades.

The color of the baby's crib, as it happened, was also a bright accent orange, like her snowsuit. It was the "debut color"—the first thing not brown or white or gray—for the "Alma Urban Mini Crib" that was bought for her, and set up against the dark-blue wall of her parents' bedroom. As with the snowsuit, one visitor after another commented on the crib. It was, it was said, so beautiful. Also orange through no particular orange affinity (or disaffinity) of the baby's mother (or father) were the lids of the baby's bottles, as well as the trim on her washcloths, and on her towel. Same orange for her small stuffed fox. The baby had an orange plastic baby spoon, and on the mixer for her food there was an orange splash cover, and an orange implement for lifting the basket of steamed food safely out. All these items were purchased fairly thoughtlessly, just in searching for "plain." Then I noticed the same orange as the trim accent color on the blue-and-white striped onesie she had received at birth and was finally growing into, and the same orange for the safety guard case around the iPhone 4 without Siri which her mother had bought post-Siri for $69.95 and had then on the first day of ownership cracked the screen of and so had unthinkingly chosen the accent color orange for the "protector." It eventually began to be difficult to not be bothered by how nice and how orange the baby's objects were. And yet also it was difficult to not want to surround the baby with objects that had been deemed, by my wedge of the zeitgeist, nice. As if taste culture could keep the baby safe. Which in some ways it could: people would subconsciously recognize that the baby belonged to the class of people to whom good things come easily, and so they would subconsciously continue to easily hand over to her the good things, like interesting jobs and educational opportunities and appealing mates, that would seem the baby's natural birthright, though of course this was an illusion. Something like that. It was an evil norm, but, again, one that it was difficult to not want to work in favor of rather than against one's own child. I would say you can see where this is going, but I feel it insufficiently gets at how much orange was arriving into the home, and how much warmth and approval these orange objects were received with by the well-educated fortunate people who encountered them. (Notably, my mother was charmed by none of it.) I at first attributed the orange overwhelm primarily to the gender-neutral color phenomenon spreading among the bohemian-brooklyn-bourgeoisie to whose taste culture I apparently belonged, though I would have wanted to maintain otherwise (a sentiment also common among that set). Orange was "modern" and "clean" and "alternative." At one point I was about to order a basic bib set for the baby and then I decided not to, because the orange was starting to feel dictatorial—the basic bibs are trimmed in orange!—and more insidious in its dictatorialness than all the pink and Disney-decorated objects selling at BuyBuy Baby and Babies R Us, all those "poor taste" objects that I was trained to treat with suspicion.

A few days after the nonbuying of the clean and modern in appearance bibs, I brought the snowsuited baby up to my institution of occasional employment, and as often happens, her snowsuit—and also her, though she was still so quiet, and I think her gray eyes seemed to strangers mostly like a screen saver on a device whose password has not yet been guessed, or a device they're not too interested in anyhow, an old model—invited comment, and someone said, as others had said, Wow I would love to have a coat like that. I had by this point become reflexively uncomfortable with how much people liked the snowsuit, though I didn't know why, and I responded with my canned comment of the coat being avalanche orange, or hunting-cap orange, to which a third person then said, No, no, it's Guantanamo orange. Everyone laughed. It was a joke. But within a second, the joke-comment seemed immediately and absolutely true, truer than the speaker had probably intended. Spring 2014 fashion in general had also been reported to have "orange as the new black," a trend most often attributed to the television show of the same name. And the timing of the orange baby object marketing, and orange as the ideal accent color, and orange as the only new color added to a line of designer home paints, followed plot-perfectly close on the wide distribution of photos of detainees at Guantanamo. And those images, instead of being straightforwardly repressed, or avoided, or addressed, had been emotionally laundered in plain sight, so that any bright vision of a radical excess of American power was hidden by being visible everywhere, among what we collectively deemed most innocent and sweet (babies) or most superfluous, a brief season of fashion, a folly. Another afternoon I see the same orange used as the detailing at a beautiful new bakery. And the new and prestigious specialized public high school being built five blocks from me has the orange color on the window frames: the accent color gives the building a clean, modern look.

More babies in art

When the baby was very small, still in what I have often heard termed the "fourth trimester," an out-of-town relative came to visit the baby, and to visit New York, and so one afternoon, the baby was put into the sling and was in this manner transported through a Magritte show at the Museum of Modern Art. The baby's sling consisted of two loops of black fabric, the one nestling into the other, and the baby was still so small that her feet didn't stick out, nothing showed of her save her bald head, and sometimes, a tiny hand gripping at the edge of the fabric. The paintings at the Magritte show included: men whose heads had been replaced by apples, a gathering of legs without bodies, an iris that was a clouded sky. Magritte-type images, naturally. Magritte's stated goal, the museum copy noted, was to make "everyday objects shriek aloud." In one exhibition room after another after another, a stranger would catch sight of the bald head, the small hand, floating amidst a vanishing cloak of sling and raincoat. One stranger after another said of the baby's inadvertent performance art, "That's my favorite piece in the show."

Sometimes it can seem like many hours with a baby

If you discovered you could communicate with a chimpanzee, would you give that up? Or would you spend near on all your hours with the other species?

Stranger danger

Some women and studies have reported to me, or to researchers, that during pregnancy they develop, alongside a heightened aversion to slightly overripe lettuce, a heightened fear of strangers. But fear of strangers is, in some cases, a euphemism. One woman confessed to me that she felt something she had never felt before, which was anxiety at night when she saw, in particular, black men on the street. She felt horrified by her own feelings. Having herself dated a black man for nine years, she said, she would have thought any primitive sense of dark-skinned people as strangers would have been eliminated. But no. Here she was, a professor who had done field studies, alone, in several central African counties, interviewing people about how they came to be involved in political violence, and regularly visited, not in a friendly way, by the local police, and through all that she had never been anxious, and now, here, alone on Amsterdam Avenue, in a New York with the lowest crime rate in years, she was worrying. However, once her baby arrived, she was, again, "cured."

How the puma affects others, three

Walking with the puma, especially when she was very young, I found that the young black men who use the drum space in my building would bless me and greet the baby, and the men working at the Pakistani restaurant around the corner would talk to the baby and talk to me, and the Yemeni man at the deli would never fail to ask after the baby, and in the immigration line when I landed in India, a man escorted me and the baby to the diplomats line, and said, This is how we treat a mother in India, and at a foreign train station an Ethiopian man walked me and the baby five minutes out of his way to the correct platform when I asked for directions, and on the subway, the construction workers whose shoulders the baby would reach out and pat, asking for their attention, would also play with the baby, and pretty much all women, everywhere, would smile at the baby. There was only one group, very demographable, to whom the baby—and myself with the baby—was suddenly invisible, and that was the group with which I am particularly comfortable, the youngish, white, well-employed, culturally literate male. There's nothing inherently commendable, or deplorable, in liking, or not liking, babies, or women with babies: it is what it is. And I encountered exceptions, in all categories. But when, without a baby, you walk by hundreds of people a day for years, and then, with a baby, you walk by hundreds of people a day for months and months, you feel you have slip-slided into another strata or you feel you have gone pre-Cambrian, or, perhaps more accurately, that you are contributing, somehow, to the next geological stratum (or both at once) and you begin to wonder what formed each geological layer, and what really was the geological layer you were in before, and what is the geological layer you are in now, and how was it that each layer seemed, individually, when you were in it, to be *everything*. Did a meteor crash, or the climate abruptly change, or a series of volcanoes erupt? I decide the baby is like a minor climate catastrophe, or, through dumb luck, redemption, and all the people who might hold out the smallest hope that a shift could result in their life on the earth being ever so slightly better feel one way about the royal catastrophe / redemption of infants, while another group that has, more or less, nowhere to go but down, on however subconscious a level, and even however much they might consciously *want* to be shifted down, also don't want to be shifted down, which is why their encounter, therefore, with the royalty of infants unavoidably bears an unwelcome message of the end of their own reign, meager or real as it may be, and so they simply avoid noticing the possibility.

Most of the great women writers of the twentieth century

Most of the great women writers of the twentieth century who write or wrote in English were or are writing from England. Or from the English commonwealth. Not as much from America. Also most of the beloved mystery novels come from England. A woman I know, who writes mysteries nowadays, mysteries that are set in Saudi Arabia and often involve a female pathologist, told me, after she sold her first mystery book, that what excited her most was having sold the book to England, where they rarely buy mysteries by Americans, being so well stocked by their own. Why are the English so drawn to mysteries? I read somewhere once—with all the diagrams and tabulations organized like cavalry—that the rise of the mystery genre in England, particularly following the Industrial Revolution, coincided with increased anxiety about social mobility. The argument pointed out, among other things, that the villains in Holmes's stories almost invariably came from the lower classes, that Moriarty (Holmes's archnemesis) has an obviously

Irish name, and that there's something supremely comforting about pinpointing a single criminal, about being able to say of a sense of evil just generally around: Here it is, the source, we have found it. Along these lines it is also noticed that the golden age of detective novels in England followed World War I, and the golden age of detective novels in Japan followed World War II. Usually the arc of the novels was a homicide, or a short series of homicides. It makes emotional sense that, among the unmysterious deaths of millions of one's countrymen, one might find it soothing to focus on a mysterious one or two. The theory may not quite hold water, but has at least a dense enough weave to keep in place a few oversized bouncy balls. Penelope Fitzgerald's first novel, *The Golden Child*, was a murder mystery set in a museum, written to entertain her husband as he was dying. Muriel Spark's third novel, *Memento Mori*, was also a murder mystery of sorts: a series of anonymous calls going out to a circle of older people, saying simply "Remember You Must Die," which of course they nearly all do, as they are old, and murdered by time.

Women writers

I have often in the past decade or so wanted to write something about "women writers," whatever that means (and whatever "about" means), but the words "women writers" seemed already to carry their own derogation (sort of like the word "ronin"), and I found the words slightly nauseating, in a way that reminded me of that fancy, innocent copy of *Little Women* that I had received as a gift as a child but could bear neither to look at nor throw out. What was I going to say? That this or that writer was not Virginia Woolf but was similarly female? That one of my favorite contemporary novels that also happened to be by a woman was *The Last Samurai* by Helen DeWitt, and that one of the things I liked about it was that it takes so many pages into the main section before you recognize the narrator's gender as female, and then so many pages more before you realize that the narrator of that section is a mother, in fact a single mother, who is trying to develop herself as a scholar and who tries to solve the problem of presenting a male role model to her son by setting him up to watch Akira Kurosawa's *Seven Samurai* over and over, a ridiculous but understandable plan, and that then the major section of the book is the son trying to solve the mystery of his paternity by investigating one potential father after another? It also seemed relevant to me that this brilliantly wordy and weird book actually sold many copies only because randomly—and I feel pretty sure about this, though I'm only guessing—there was a Tom Cruise film by the same title that came out around the same time as the book. I had so many little artifacts like this that seemed to point to … I didn't know what they pointed to. I had a strong feeling that I couldn't see the contemporary situation, and I decided that this was because firsthand knowledge is an obstacle to insight. What of the other artifacts? There were those forgotten American noir women, like Evelyn Piper of *Bunny Lake Is Missing* and Dorothy Hughes of *In A Lonely Place* and Vera Caspary of *Laura* (and thirty-eight other novels) and Patricia Highsmith, less forgotten, of one terrifying betrayal after another, and these oddities, and their odd obscurity, seemed to cluster around … something. As did the fact that the Feminist Press had reissued many of these books, which were otherwise out of print, and I wouldn't have come across them save their placement on certain remainders tables. (I also felt that *Gone Girl* took most of its plot from Caspary's *The Man Who Loved*

His Wife.) Why so much crime? Why so many mysteries? Why was my copy of *The Collected Works of Jane Bowles* part of the Out-of-Print Masterworks series? The same was true of my copy of *Mrs. Caliban* by Rachel Ingalls, a perfect novel about a neglected housewife in love with a giant escaped lizard man.

And then there was the fact that contemporary crime fiction coming out of Japan is written mostly by women, and that when I had wanted to write a profile of the Japanese writer Natsuo Kirino, the author of the bestselling *Out*—about four women who work in a bento factory and become involved in a series of murders of men whom they have to dispose of by cutting them apart like sushi—I was told that she was very private, didn't give interviews, and that the publication of her next book in English had been canceled because she was just so difficult to work with. I was enamored with a story by Kono Taeko called "Toddler Hunting" about a woman who goes to great lengths to buy other people's little boys beautiful sweaters that she then is obsessed with watching them struggle into and out of. I even had in my mind a list of male writers that I thought were somehow "female" on the page—Walser, Kafka, Kleist, for some reason all German-language—which made me realize that maybe I just meant writers that I really liked in a way that had something to do with the volume of certain kinds of quiet. I wanted to line up all the baubles and bothers and clusters and … but in the end, all the lining up of these almost-things got me to thinking of one of the more hauntingly ridiculous passages in Claude Lévi-Strauss's *Tristes Tropiques*, where he attributes Christopher Columbus's mistaking of squids for mermaids to an "error in taste." "This was before people saw things as belonging to a whole," he clarifies. I had to let the "women writers" go. Better to just let things accrete, like the rust on the vats at the rum distilleries Levi-Strauss visits in another chapter; rusty vats make much better rum, he says, and I find I trust him.

Near the end of *Life Among the Savages* by Shirley Jackson—a writer most remembered for her story about a civic group of people stoning to death their fellow citizen—the narrator is expecting her fourth child; her children and husband are asking after the not-yet-born baby daily; the narrator is trying to get a reprieve from the topic. "I took my coffee into the dining room and settled down with the morning paper. A woman in New York had had twins in a taxi. A woman in Ohio had just had her seventeenth child. A twelve-year-old girl in Mexico had given birth to a thirteen-pound boy. The lead article on the woman's page was about how to adjust the older child to the new baby. I finally found an account of an axe murder on page seventeen, and held my coffee cup up to my face to see if the steam might revive me."

For many years, Shirley Jackson was nearly the only "woman writer" I had read. Then, around age twenty-five, I had the blunt experience of looking at my bookshelves and noticing that my bookshelves were filled almost exclusively with books by men. Which was fine, I wasn't going to get in a rage about it, I loved those books that I had read. But I was unsettled, since my bookshelves meant either there were no good books by women, or I had somehow read in such a way as to avoid them all. I had never had my Jane Austen phase, or Edith Wharton phase, or even George Eliot phase, I associated those writers with puberty, or "courting," both things which repelled me. (I now know I was stupid to feel that way.) But, like I said, I wasn't going to rage at myself, or at the world, I was just going to try to read some books by women. But where to start? I came across a book by someone named Denis Johnson. (I didn't run in a bookish crowd.) Graspingly, I thought that Yes, I was pretty sure that I had heard that this Denis—I was imagining a French woman, or maybe a French-Canadian—was very good. There was no author photo on the book. The first Denis Johnson book I read was called *The Name of the World*, a sort of rewrite of a Bernhard novel; it centered on a man who goes to look at the same painting in a museum every day and the reader eventually learns that the man's wife and child died in a car accident. I liked the book, though upon finishing it, I did find myself reflecting that it was surprising that this particular book was by a woman, but I dismissed that thought, because it's always so unpleasant—so distasteful!—to think about the gender of who wrote a book—shouldn't it ideally be anyone? Maybe it had been textbook self-defense, or self-loathing, that had kept me from reading books by women. The only "girl" book that made it through to me—also a gift, from my childhood best friend's mother—was *Anne of Green Gables*, that book that is mysteriously so beloved in Japan that there are direct flights from Tokyo to Prince Edward Island, the tiny green patch the fictional redhead is from.

Still: I kept clumsily seeking out books by women. (*The Pillow Book* and *The Tale of Genji* were finds in that awkward search.) When I discovered how brilliant Muriel Spark's novels were—they also were mostly out of print when I found them—I did feel a bit of fury—an emotion I nearly always deny myself—but that was that. (My daughter's middle name is Spark.) And yet I had never envied men their literary place, and I still don't, and I had never envied men much of anything, ever ... until very recently. I now envy men, but for just one thing. What thing? It is true that at the moment the baby is beating a small wooden cutting board against the ground, that the cutting board had at one point had on it an apricot I had sliced into tiny bits for her, she has since sat on some, and smashed some into the ground, she has taken a lengthy interest in my wallet, she has held the supermarket-discount-points card at a distance, then put it in her mouth, then held it at a distance away again, she has not yet learned to crawl but can drag herself across the floor to the edge of a set of stairs I am hoping to keep her from exploring further, she has gathered fuzz from the shag rug here at this rental cabin that has been obtained as a luxuriously imagined Room of One's Own, she has been interested in having her hand inside of my mouth, and has not been interested in lying down, she is now trying to pull herself up along a ledge and is now trapped in a position from which she can discover no out and so requires rescue by the large being (me) who is always with her, later she needs rescue simply from being on her stomach, and so in brief moments, between these activities, I have one-third of an associative thought, about that story "Pregnancy Diary" by Yoko Ogawa in which a woman's sister is pregnant and very nauseous throughout the pregnancy and the narrator begins making grapefruit jam for her nauseous sister, and the sister loves it, it's the only thing she can bear to eat, and so the narrator keeps making it even though she read a sign at the grocery store that the grapefruit was not safe, and so she believes she has ruined the baby … but really I'm insufficiently upset about not being able to think, and then the baby falls asleep. She sleeps on her back, slightly tossed to the side, with both arms in the same direction, like she's in a boat I can't see. Her breathing in this moment is making her glow like an amulet. I had been talking about gender envy. The one thing I envy. The first gender-envy thoughts I have had really in my entire life started maybe not immediately following the arrival of the puma in my apartment, but shortly after, when the puma spent a lot of time spinning a wooden cookie on a rod, or maybe shortly after that, when I took her for her first swim in a pool and she persisted uncomplainingly even as it began to rain. The envious thought was simply that a man can have a baby that their romantic partner doesn't know about. This is a crazy thought, of course, but I find myself feeling it with such sincerity that I cannot see its edges. The thought seems a descendant of a thought I had while hoping to become pregnant, which was imagining a woman who was pregnant with twins but didn't have the courage to confess this to her partner, who she believes will be devastated by the news, and so she dreams up plans to come up with some "hysterical" reason for not wanting her partner there for the birth, and then what? What will she do with the second child? Raise it in secrecy? I knew I wouldn't be having a second baby. And while I of course felt terrible for that secret child of Arnold Schwarzenegger who—I am presuming, I refuse to research the misery of others—had grown up for years either not knowing who his real father was, or knowing that he had to keep as a secret who his real father was—still I envied Schwarzenegger. I had considered envying men before—I pretend to envy things like their higher incidence of ungrounded confidence and mono-mania, but I don't really envy those things, and I'm not sure I even believe in them—but this, the covert-baby-having thing, was the first real thing.

Baby girls and men

On up until I was about thirty, I had a strong preference for men over women. I mean specifically as friends, as people to talk to. If a male and a female exactly alike were to enter a room, in my deformed perceptions the male was magnified into glory. It wasn't until this primitive preference began to expire, for whatever reasons, that it began to bother me that it had previously existed. I didn't blame my mother for this trait, but I did feel that I had inherited it from her. Despite my having a mother who is extremely intelligent and capable and giving, I still grew up with a sense that it was always nicest to be around men, and I decided that maybe this dated back to my mother's father having died before she was born, and her mother then being alone, with two young girls, in the household of her in-laws, and there being no male taking his place, ever, and so this atmosphere of any room being short a male seemed to have been passed on to me, and then, when my father similarly was suddenly gone, this atmosphere thickened … until it lifted. Or at least lifted for me. Did it ever lift for my mother?

When I saw how fully she fell in love with the puma, I felt that the both of us had fallen in love with a girl in some healthy, unprecedented way. My mother recently sent me a text that read: "I love the channels between 210–223. Amazing information/world views. They just said that Chelsea's husband runs a hedge fund that lost 40 percent since he bet the wrong way on the Euro crisis, then they went on to bad-mouth him—you create a job for him and pour money into it since Chelsea was unable to get any better husband for herself." Was this my old mother (and self)? Shortly thereafter my mother followed up this text with: "Doubt it is true about not getting a husband, she looks pretty good on TV. I think it was a malicious angry comment of the commentator."

A *friend who is not a close friend*

A friend who is not a close friend was trying to get pregnant, via in vitro fertilization, on her own. She had health issues that led doctors to tell her that her chances were low. I didn't know whether to ask or not ask how it was going. I didn't ask. Then she informed me and others, via e-mail, that she was six weeks pregnant, happily. I'm not very good with time, with noting where I am in it, or how much of it has passed, but time proceeded and I began to accumulate anxiety about still not having heard of a birth. I woke from a dream one night, a straightforward dream, in which I learned that she had lost the baby. I felt sure I had had a vision. But in real life she hadn't lost the baby. Three days later I received an e-mail announcing that the baby had been born. The announcement came on the same day as one of the more important rulings in favor of gay marriage.

This friend was not the only woman I knew who had decided to have a baby on her own. Within the span of a single year, five women I knew had deliberately had babies on their own, without a partner, or in one case, with a partner who was a friend who wanted to be involved, though there was no romantic connection. Prior to these five women I had known only one woman who had had a baby on her own, deliberately. This was an older cousin of mine, and for her it had been such a remarkable decision that no one had thought it appropriate to remark upon it, and one of the only reasons the awkwardness around her had gone away was because at nearly eight months the baby had died inside the womb, and then, though she was over forty, she became pregnant again, and the second time around, the baby was carried to term, and the then radicalness of her decision paled against joy and relief. Now it seems there are many more varieties of "normal" family.

I never

I never especially cared for babies. When I heard about babies dying there was a part of myself that thought, At least it's not a child! A child is someone that people know and who knows other people; was the loss of a baby really so different from the loss of a potential baby that happened every month? Once, at an elementary-school-age summer camp, they took us young campers to do rubbings of gravestones. My friend took several rubbings of the gravestones of babies, with the birth and death dates sometimes in the same month. Then she had written sad, short Blakean poems about the babies. After that, I thought that she was an odd girl, and melodramatic. I don't feel that way now.

A Doll's House

I once saw a production of Ibsen's *A Doll's House* in which all the characters except for Nora were played by small people, by a midget, a dwarf, a person with Williams syndrome ... This made stark the power that the child-like Nora, the wife and mother, really did have. I can still hear the enormous woman asking her very small and angry husband for some chocolates.

However I have only heard of and seen one performance of *The Doll's House* in which, at a certain moment, the audience literally gasped—and it was not at this version but at a straightforward performance. The gasp came when, in the second act, a real live baby was brought onto the stage. I don't think even a live bear would have elicited as much of a reaction; I once saw a magic show in a theater and at the end of the show a live elephant showed up on stage, and I can report that the reaction to the elephant was considerably less than the reaction to the baby. Why was the baby on stage such a force? Because it might cry? Maybe it was the simple thrill of cameo: a baby seems indisputably from everyday life, and everyday life, though depicted on stage, also feels conspicuously absent from it. The actors other than the baby, if the baby can be termed an actor simply by context, seemed suddenly neon in their falseness, which in turn made them seem real, as if visible backstage, brushing their teeth, watching *Mad Men* on a laptop. In the original Ibsen script, there is no baby, there are just young children.

People who get along well with babies

Four women are having dinner together. One begins to tell of how well her mother gets along with her baby, her grandson. The woman's mother, the grandmother, prepares Hungarian food for the baby, she prepares him chicken with walnuts and pomegranate in rice which is then stuffed into a pepper—he loves it. The mother's mother also has things to say to the baby all day long, she is in a constant conversation with him, she doesn't run out of spirit to talk to him, and he loves it, and, because she talks to him so much, and cares for him so much, she is also the best at getting him to laugh; he loves her; she loves him. "I even believe," the friend says, "that when me and my sister were babies, she was also this good." Another mother at the table (who is, naturally, also a daughter) has her mother living with her right now, for a few months, as she helps take care of her granddaughter, now a young girl, no longer a baby. The grandmother is good with the young girl, very good, but maybe she was even better with her when she was a baby. When she was a baby, she was amazing with her, and she was a difficult baby, a colicky baby. This grandmother is wonderful with babies, and with the very elderly, she is wonderful with the extremely vulnerable, it is observed, she cheerfully anticipates their needs, even as, with the not very vulnerable, she can be, actually, quite difficult. I then shared a story, about my own grandmother, a woman who is not noted for her sunny disposition, not at all, but who also, like these other noted women, is really wonderful with babies; she raised her grandchildren, and even helped raise her great-grandchildren, when they were tiny. Even now, her great-grandson, a toddler—his favorite activity is to bring his great-grandmother her cane. My mother also takes babies very seriously, loves them, and when I return home after having left the baby with her, I never find them separated, either the baby is asleep on my mother's chest, or she is sitting right next to her on the sofa, gesturing. And so on.

Then I notice that somehow we speak suspiciously of people whom we describe as getting along unusually well with babies. As if they do not get along with adults. And I realize that I have become someone who gets along unusually well with babies too. And that I miss my baby, and am desperate to leave to return home to her.

The beginning of misunderstanding

I sometimes feel, as a mother, that there is no creature I better understand than my child. This is probably because she can't really say anything. I am beginning to worry, as she is just beginning to speak, that we are entering the beginning of misunderstanding. (Though I understand that it is likely that before it was only a misunderstanding that led me to think I understood.) Her words are: bubble, ten, shoes, mama, papa, eyes, up, and encore. A writer once said to me of his two children, "I found that once they started to speak, my friends lost all interest in them. Before they spoke, it seemed like they might be thinking anything. Then they learned language and it turned out they just had a list of wants and dissatisfactions." It's as if babies don't grow larger but instead smaller, at least in our perception. It's striking that in the canonical Gospels, we meet Jesus as a baby and as an adult, but as a child and teenager, he is unserviceable.

A *new citizen*

When the puma was three weeks old, I brought her to the post office to apply for her passport. I brought along her birth certificate, her social security card, a photocopy of my passport, a photocopy of her dad's passport, a notarized form signed by her dad indicating that he granted permission for his daughter to apply for a passport without his being present—I had done the research. For good measure, I brought along not one but two sets of passport photos that had been taken at a professional passport photo–taking location. Taking those photos had taken awhile. The puma had to appear in the photo alone, against a blank white wall, which sounds like a reasonable set of requirements. But the puma was not yet able to hold up her head, let alone sit, and she also did not excel at being awake, and her eyes needed to be open, and looking at the camera—these are the requirements of any passport photo—and, so, it took a while.

Then the line for the passport application window at the post office was also very long.

At the passport application teller window, the man in front of me was dismissed because, although he had a photocopy of the front of his driver's license, he did not have a photocopy of the back.

I approached the teller window and passed our paperwork through the opening beneath the bulletproof shield. The puma and I had waited about forty-five minutes to get there. I felt very good about getting this essential task done. Our paperwork was immediately handed back; the teller impassively stated: "No, her hand is obstructing her chin, this photo is unusable."

She did have her hand near her mouth. Triumphantly, I indicated that there were two sets of photos, that her hand was not on her chin in the other set.

"No, we can see the mother's hand in these photos."

"But of course my hand is there, I had to hold her up against the background."

We were dismissed.

The next week there was a shutdown of the government.

I was trying to get the passport done in time for travel I had to do for work.

I then took many photos of the puma with my iPhone, having read online that this could be done: all one needed was to then find a place that could print the photos passport-sized. So I took the modern technology object to a Staples, but they were unable to help, and then to a Kinko's but they were unable to help, and so then I went back to the original FedEx office where the unacceptable passport photos had been taken; their passport photo camera equipment was broken. We then went to a souvenir and electronics and passport-photos-taken-here storefront. Working there was one immigrant from Bangladesh, one from Mexico, and one from Pakistan. They knew all about the issue of not having a parent's hand or arm visible in the passport photo. They hid my hand behind a scarf and had me kneel down on the floor and then hold up the baby like a puppet in front of the white backdrop. I and the puma were both very hungry by this time. But the passport window was only open until 2:30 p.m., so we headed right over to the line.

The woman behind the bulletproof glass said she was going to lunch.

"But the sign says this window is open from 9:00 a.m. to 4:00 p.m."

The woman said she had already waited an hour longer than she had intended to go to lunch and now she was going to go to lunch.

We continued on to a second post office. No one was available who had the training to handle passports.

At a third post office, again, no one was available, we were told. Then a woman emerged from a back room with a sandwich in her hand; she said she was available until 3:00 p.m.; it was 2:50 p.m. She forsook her sandwich to help us out. She went through our paperwork piece by piece. She got to the photos. She took out a ruler and began taking measurements of the likeness of the puma's face. "Her head is too small," she said. "Way too small." It was, she specified, two millimeters too small. "Listen, since September 11, they are very careful with these passport applications, this will never pass."

We went, so hungry, to a CVS on 42nd Street and 10th Avenue. A woman in line in front of us was discussing with the teller how she had five sets of visa photos taken, she was trying to get her visa to China, but she had doubts about this newest set of photos, too. I felt I was about to lose it, standing in line, listening to the conversation whose end was not yet imaginable, and I probably would have gotten angry, or wept, had my mood not been preempted by the puma getting angry, and weeping. Finally a screen was pulled down. The puma's photo was taken, a face of resigned despair. We paid double, so as to get two sets of photos, one with the puma's head on the larger side, one on the smaller. We returned to the original post office. The fluorescent lighting seemed to have turned to sound. We handed over the paperwork. The photo was fine! The xerox of my mother's passport was fine. The xerox of the father's passport was fine. The social security card was more than was needed. The notarized form signed by the father was fine. The form was notarized with a driver's license, not with a passport. Did we have that driver's license with us? We were sent away.

Her passport didn't make it through in time for her first meager trip at eight weeks old, across the border to Canada. We just argued her way across the border. Then returning was trickier. Border patrol was unimpressed with our birth certificate and social security card. "There are no photos here," the woman at the booth said. "How can I know if this baby is the baby you say she is if there's not a photo of her to confirm her identity?" We looked at her. Eventually her supervisor let us through. It had to be acknowledged, that picture or no picture, no one could identify the baby, except for us.

Money and babies

My mother takes the chicken—when she began to loco-
mote, she ceased being a puma and became a chicken—
out with her one evening. The two of them attend a dinner held at my mother's synagogue, in the basement, one
of these organized-by-age dinners, this is the over-forty
social group, which means that most of the people who
attend are over sixty. The chicken walks around the table,
carrying her winter pants here and there, offering them
to diners, rescinding her offer, and more. After the dinner, my mother tells me that she should charge $1,000
a day to bring the chicken to a nursing home, because a
baby offers so much happiness and healing, being near a
baby is good for one's health, it is much better than blue
algae or Prozac—it is amazing.

The chicken's dad then said to my mom that Yes, he
agrees. In fact, that is his take on babysitting. That you
charge people $20 an hour for the privilege of being with
the baby. A baby is a goldmine.

Everything they said was true, and yet also, we know,
not the case.

American Innovations

'Strikingly beautiful'
Guardian

'Hopeful, funny and innovative'
Independent

'Thrilling'
New Yorker

'Rivka Galchen is one of the best things going.
She writes for the joy of it and so artfully, and conforms
to no one else's standards'
RACHEL KUSHNER

'Like the pinball wizard of American letters, with a
narrative voice that can ricochet from wonder to terror
to hilarity … The delicacy and brilliance of what Galchen
is doing doesn't yet have a name'
KAREN RUSSELL

There are many strange things in *American Innovations*:
a young woman's furniture walks out on her; a student of
Library Sciences develops a third breast; refrigerated string
cheese won't stay put and time travel features prominently.
Most strange is this wonderworld's familiarity. Each told from
the perspective of a modern woman attuned to and under
attack by the small ironies and psychological perversities of
everyday life, these eye-opening, pitch-perfect, exhilarating
stories soon seem far more real than what we call real life.

Atmospheric Disturbances

'Genuinely suspenseful, fresh and wry,
Galchen is a writer to be watched'
Economist

'Playful and moving'
Daily Telegraph

'Original and affecting'
New Yorker

'A powerful novel about love, longing, Doppler radar
and the true appreciation of a nice cookie with your tea.
Atmospheric Disturbances is fantastic'
NATHAN ENGLANDER

'Playful yet profound, Murakami-esque yet original,
analytical yet heartbreaking, an absolutely stunning
and unforgettable debut'
VENDELA VIDA

When Dr. Leo Liebenstein's wife disappears, she leaves behind a single confounding clue: a woman who looks, talks, and behaves exactly like her. A simulacrum. But Leo is not fooled, and he knows better than to trust his senses in matters of the heart. Certain that the real Rema is alive and in hiding, he embarks on a quixotic journey to reclaim her. With the help of his psychiatric patient Harvey – who believes himself to be a secret agent able to control the weather – his investigation leads him from the streets of New York City to the southernmost reaches of Patagonia, in search of the woman he loves.